# One Word Can Change the World

*journal belongs to...*

© 2017 Ranch House Press
All rights reserved. Printed in the United States of America.

www.annettebridges.com

ISBN: 978-1-946371-21-8

Here is a list of one-word prompts to get your started. How do these words make you feel? What are the first thoughts that come to you? Words are powerful and each and every word has the power to change your world — your mood, your motivation, your memories. Continue this list with "one words" that are meaningful to you or you are curious about or you simply what to ponder their meaning to your life.

**Journal Prompts**

*One Word can change the World*

1. Happiness
2. Love
3. Light
4. Dream
5. Believe
6. Hope
7. Dare
8. Choose
9. Beach
10. Forgiveness
11. Heart
12. Be
13. Passion
14. Today
15. Pause
16. Breathe
17. Simple
18. Intuition
19. Ready
20. Age
21. Wandering
22. Goals
23. Playful
24. Travel
25. Why
26. Desire
27. Wish
28. Stretch
29. Adventure
30. Fun

*color your world*

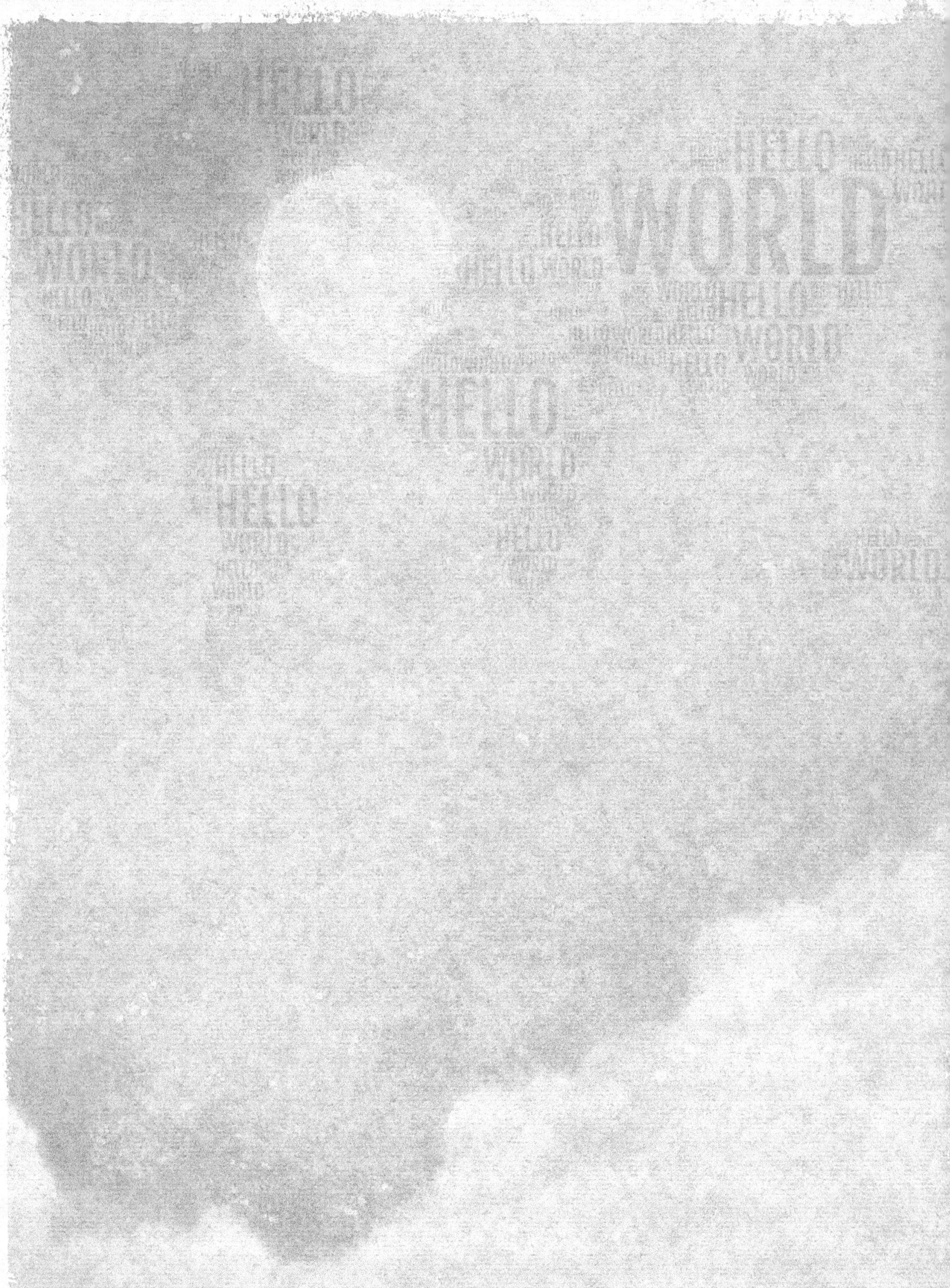
HELLO
WORLD
HELLO
WORLD

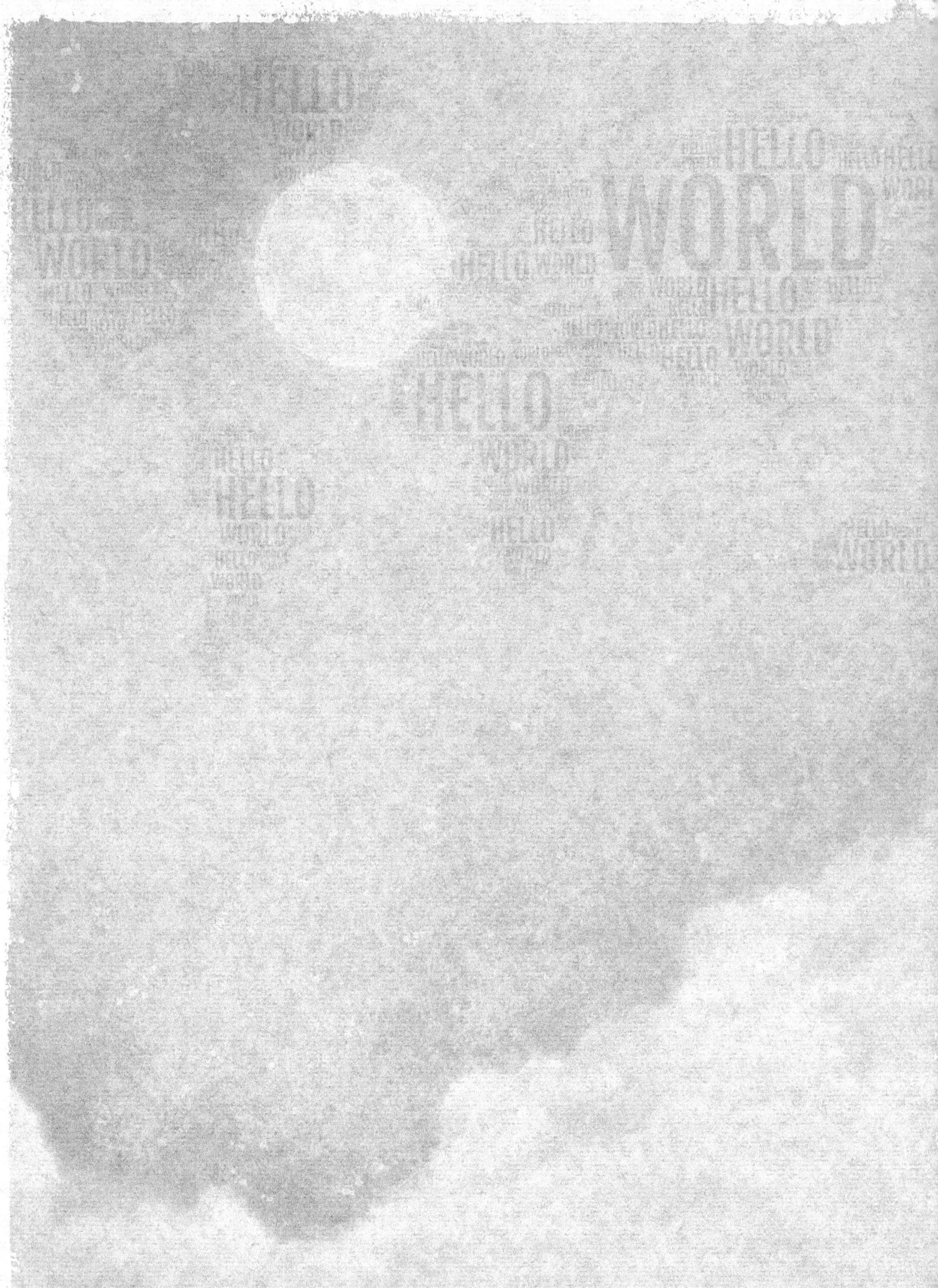
HELLO
WORLD

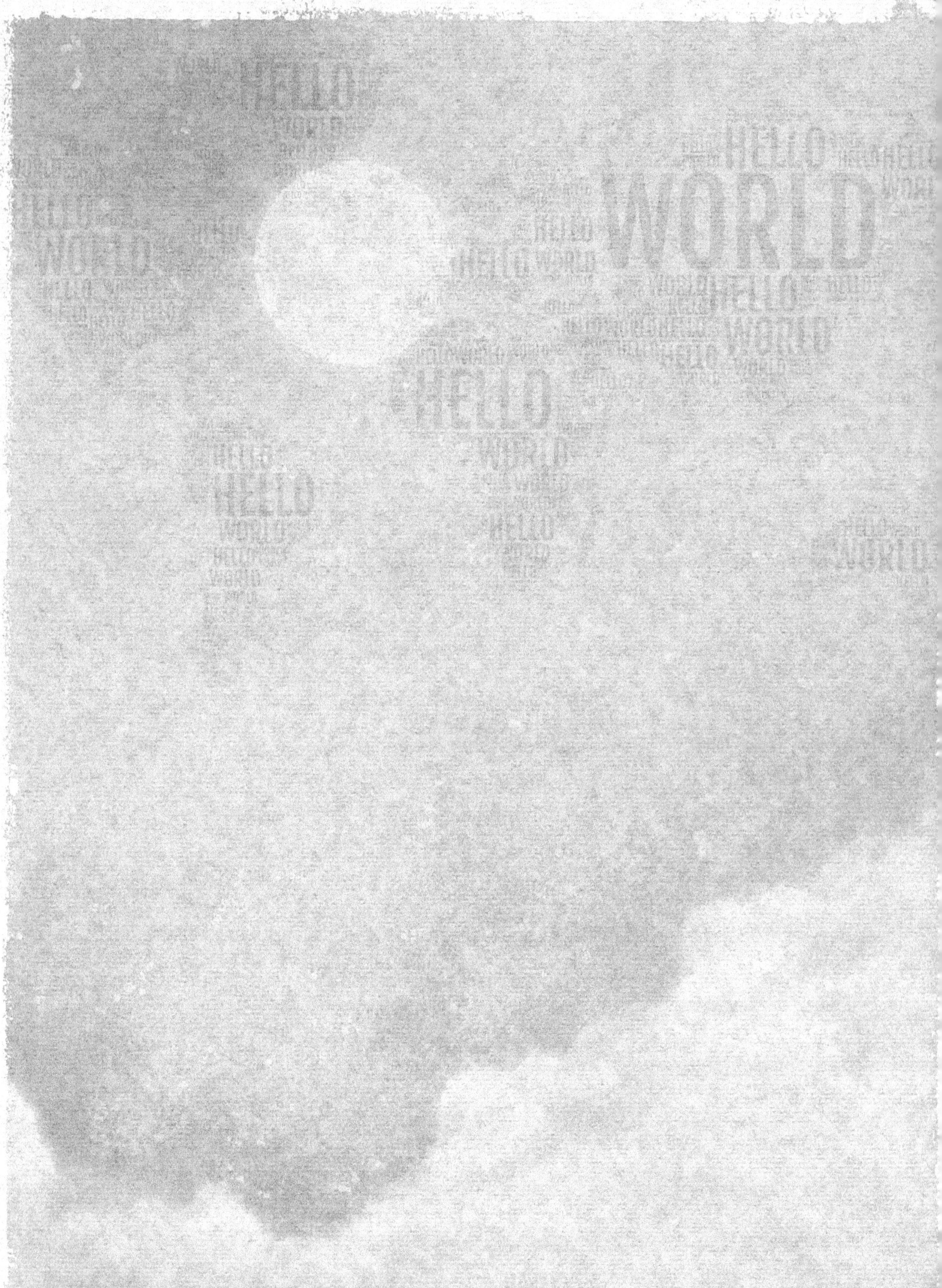
HELLO
WORLD

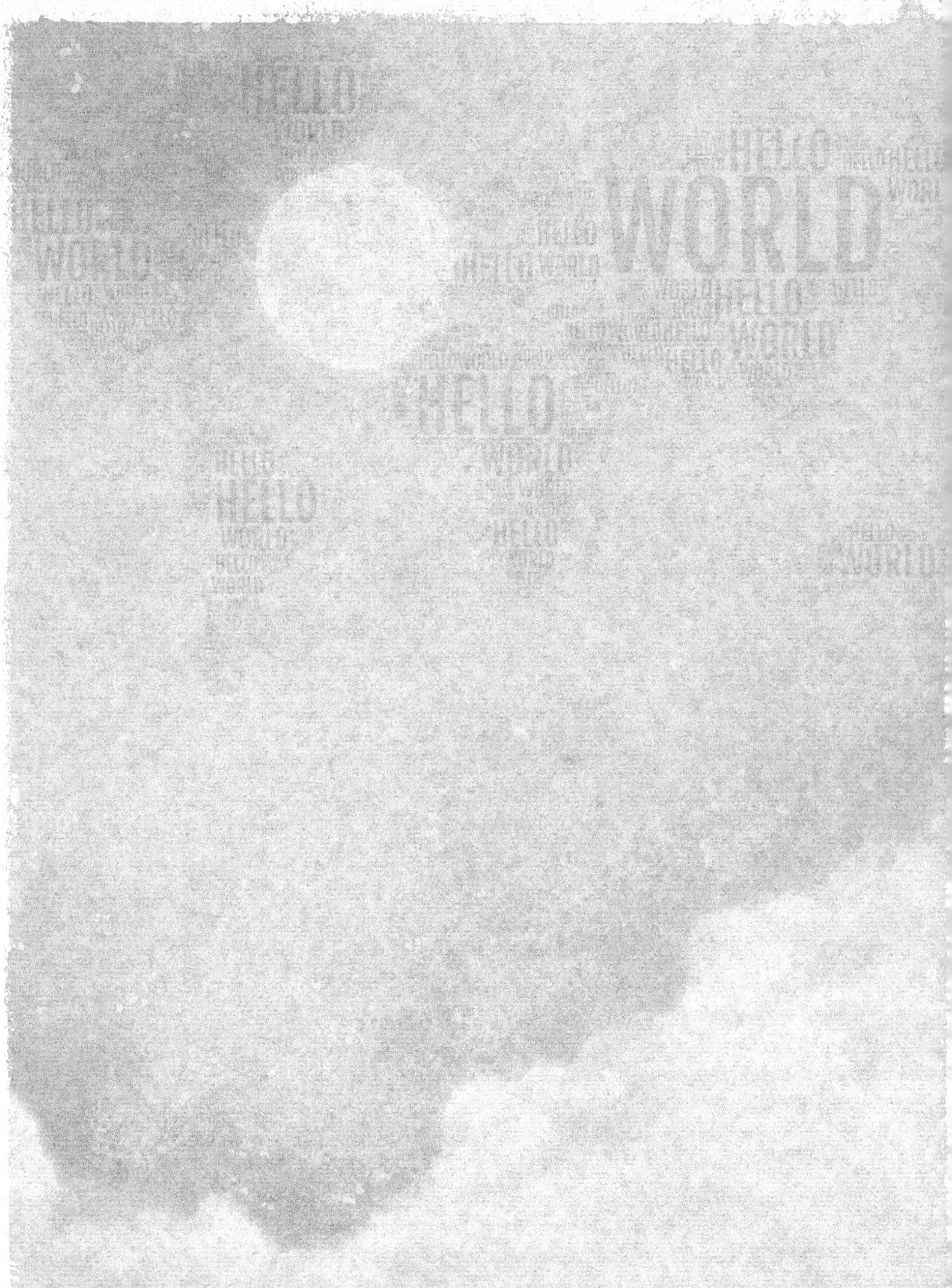
HELLO
WORLD

WORLD
HELLO
WORLD
HELLO
WORLD
HELLO
WORLD

# ABOUT the CREATOR

**Annette Bridges** is an author, publisher and women's retreat host on a mission to help every woman realize her story is extraordinary, valuable and noteworthy.

She has published the *Color Your World Journal Series* and formed a journal club to provide community, support and tools for women to record their ideas, feelings, experiences, memories and all the important details of their lives.

Before writing books and publishing journals and coloring books, this former public school and homeschool educator spent a decade writing hundreds of helpful, instructive, and light-hearted columns published by Texas newspapers, parenting magazines, websites and bloggers.

Annette lives on a Texas cattle ranch with her husband John, dachshund Lady and lots of cows. She can drive a tractor but only if wearing a fresh coat of lipstick and it's not her pedicure day!

You can learn more about Annette's books and products, blogs and videos as well as her women's retreats and other events at www.annettebridges.com.

Look for her on social media, too!

# MESSAGE from the PUBLISHER

The *Color Your World Journal Series* is a pathway to self-discovery. It's where you write notes to yourself. Be your own cheerleader. Give yourself encouragement. Tell yourself what you're grateful for. Celebrate you!

There are countless reasons to keep a journal including collecting favorite recipes, listing goals and celebrating every experience and every one that's near and dear to you. A journal provides a home for the memories and lessons learned that you never want to forget.

## Why a niche journal?

If you're anything like me, you have a journal (or even two or three journals) where you write anything and everything about anything and everything. My challenge comes when trying to find something I've written. I flip and flip through the pages of my two, three or four journals trying to find whatever it is. I never remember which journal I wrote down my whatever's!!

The solution? A niche journal! A journal that has a specific focus and theme! A journal where you can record your ideas, inspirations and things you want to remember in the appropriate journal.

## Why big unlined paper?

Because big unlined paper is needed to record big ideas, dreams and memories! You need room to grow, stretch and expand. You need space to think beyond the confines of what you've always done, to pursue new dreams, discover your power and reimagine your purpose again and again. You need pages without lines and limitations to reconnect with your creative, perfectly imperfect self.

Plus, big unlined paper gives you space for more than words. You have plenty of room to doodle, draw or post photographs and clippings, too.

## Why color is important?

When you journal, use colored pens and markers! Your world doesn't happen in black and white. Your life should be lived and written about in many colors. Even dark and sad memories feel lighter and brighter when told in color.

Journaling in color affects your mood and perception of your world. Colors evoke calm, cheer and comfort. Using color can lift your spirit and inspire your imagination. You may be surprised by all the beautiful benefits from adding more color into your life story.

When journaling, give yourself time to listen to your heart and reflect. Breathe in the moments. Feel. Be quiet. Let yourself be totally and thoroughly present with your thoughts. Let your heart transform you and teach you new insights. Open your mind to consider new ideas and possibilities. You may find that what your heart teaches will be life changing.